This book belongs to

....

First published 2011 by Brown Watson
The Old Mill, 76 Fleckney Road,
Kibworth Beauchamp, Leic LE8 0HG

ISBN: 978-0-7097-1920-5

© 2011 Brown Watson, England
Reprinted 2011, 2012, 2013, 2014 twice, 2015, 2017, 2018, 2020

Printed in Malaysia

My Little Book of
Prayers

Additional prayers by Gill Davies

Brown Watson
ENGLAND

The Lord's Prayer

Our Father, who art in heaven,
Hallowed be thy name;
Thy kingdom come;
Thy will be done,
On earth as it is in heaven.
Give us this day our daily bread.
And forgive us our trespasses,
As we forgive them that trespass against us.
And lead us not into temptation;
But deliver us from evil.
For thine is the kingdom,
The power, and the glory,
Forever and ever.

AMEN.

Now, Before I Run to Play

Now, before I run to play,
Let me not forget to pray
To God who kept me through the night
And waked me with the morning light.

Help me, Lord, to love thee more
Than I ever loved before,
In my work and in my play
Be thou with me through the day.

AMEN.

TRADITIONAL

Today is a New Day

Today is a new day
And a chance to try once more,
To be as good as we are able
And kinder than before.

Today we pray that we shall behave,
Not stamp or squabble or shout,
But be God's children the way He likes,
Helping each other out.

We don't mean to be so selfish;
Or to do things that are wrong:
Please, God, help us to love each other
And show us how to get along.

Family

I thank you, God, that I was born
Into a happy family.
Please take care of all those children
Not so fortunate as me.
I know that while I'm laughing,
Other children may be sad,
Hungry, lonely, lost, or ill
So I am so very glad
That I am well and happy,
With time for work and play;
I have a family that cares for me
And loves me every day.
I pray my life will stay so blessed
But meanwhile wish to share
A little of my joy
With those who need more care.

God is Watching Me

I know that God is watching me,
So I try hard not to cry,
But would He hug me if I did
And say, "I'll help you if you try"?

That is what my mother does
And my father helps me too;
So, please, God, are my parents
Like little bits of you?

Praise God From Whom
All Blessings Flow

Praise God, from whom all blessings flow;
Praise Him, all creatures here below;
Praise Him above, ye heavenly host:
Praise Father, Son, and Holy Ghost.

AMEN.

TRADITIONAL

Thank You

Thank you for the petals,
And the blossom on the tree.
Thank you for the blue, blue sky
And the sun that shines on me.

Thank you for beautiful snowflakes,
Like stars falling from the sky.
I should like to hold them in my hand
But they vanish when I try.

Thank you for the gentle rain
That helps the grass stay green.
Thank you, God, for everything
That I have ever seen.

12

Friends

Thank you, God, for all my friends
I am so happy they're here today,
To share my games and laughter,
To talk and sing and dance and play.

We all need each other's support:
Jesus, You helped the lonely, sick and sad.
Help me to see what my friends need,
And be there to make them glad.

I can laugh with them and chatter
And work the school day through,
Knowing I am not alone
For my best friends include You.

A Wonderful World

Flowers, trees, rain and sun,
Laughter, friends and having fun.
The world is a wonderful place to be
So, thank you, God, for making me.

Help

When Noah built the Ark
He rescued lions, bears and even bees;
God saw him safely through the storm
But now today He rescues me.
If I were crossing the Red Sea,
God would make the waters part;
If I were the shepherd, David,
God would put music in my heart.

Please make me as brave as Daniel
Who tamed the lions in the den;
Please make me as wise as Solomon
As strong as Samson, Ruth, and then
Help me to help all others –
Just as the Bible says we should;
Help me to try my very best
To be kind and brave and good.

Jesus is Real

Jesus, You were born in a stable.
How I wish I were there that night,
To see the shepherds and the angels
And the kings and the star so bright.
And I wish I could have been with You
When you walked across the sea.

And I wish when You chose Your special friends
That one of them had been me!
But the grown-ups say You are still here;
When I pray, You listen and see
So I can be one of Your chosen friends,
You are as close as close can be.

God in Heaven

God in heaven hear my prayer,
Keep me in thy loving care.
Be my guide in all I do,
Bless all those who love me too.

AMEN.

TRADITIONAL

Lamb of God, I look to Thee

Lamb of God, I look to Thee;
Thou shalt my example be;
Thou art gentle, meek, and mild,
Thou wast once a little child.

Fain I would be as Thou art:
Give me Thy obedient heart.
Thou art pitiful and kind:
Let me have Thy loving mind.

Loving Jesus, gentle Lamb,
In Thy gracious hands I am;
Make me, Saviour, what Thou art,
Live Thyself within my heart.

I shall then show forth Thy praise,
Serve Thee all my happy days;
Then the world shall always see
Christ, the holy Child, in me.

AMEN.

TRADITIONAL

Playing

Playing is so important;
We need to stretch our legs and run,
To throw balls and chase and jump,
In the warmth of the glowing sun.

Do you smile, God, when we are playing?
For You made us to be like You
So thanks for laughter and happy things
And fun the whole year through.

Jesus Was a Little Boy

Jesus, You were a little boy
Once, so very long ago.
Can You remember how it felt?
I am sure You can – and so,
Please help me to be good;
Remind me I am not alone –
Even when I'm naughty
And make my parents groan.
So, especially on those horrid days
When everything goes wrong,
Remember, You were small too, once,
And do help me to be strong.

Father Hear My Prayer

Father in heaven hear my prayer.
Keep me in your love and care.
Be my guide in all I do.
Bless all those who love me too.

AMEN.

TRADITIONAL

Thank You, God

Thank You, God, for this good food
That keeps me strong and growing fast,
For delicious tastes I can enjoy
And water always in my glass.

Thank You for friends and family
Who share this meal – and now we pray,
Please help those many who are hungry
And may not eat at all today.

We Thank Thee, Lord

We thank Thee, Lord, for happy hearts,
For rain and sunny weather.
We thank Thee, Lord, for this our food,
And that we are together.

TRADITIONAL

Tomorrow I Shall be Good

I pray that tomorrow I shall be good
And do the things I really should.
I shall not be naughty, or rude or bad
Or do anything that makes God sad.

So I pray, please, God, help me to be
The good little child You want to see.
It is hard to be perfect all day through
But I shall do my best to behave like You.

At the Close of Every Day

At the close of every day,
Lord, to Thee I kneel and pray.
Look upon Thy little child,
Look in love and mercy mild.
O forgive and wash away
All my naughtiness this day,
And both when I sleep and wake
Bless me for my Saviour's sake.

AMEN.

TRADITIONAL

Matthew, Mark, Luke and John

Matthew, Mark, Luke and John,
Bless the bed that I lie on.
Four corners to my bed,
Four angels round my head.
One to watch and one to pray,
And two to bear my fears away.
I see the moon, and the moon sees me.
God bless the moon, and God bless me.

The sky is so big and the stars so bright
I know God is watching me tonight.
I pray that He keeps me safe as I sleep
Just as shepherds watch their sheep.

TRADITIONAL

Dear Father in Heaven

Dear Father in heaven,
Look down from above;
Bless papa and mama,
And those whom I love.

May angels guard over
My slumbers, and when
The morning is breaking,
Awake me.

AMEN.

TRADITIONAL